Sufism
and
Faith

Nader Angha

Pir, Oveyssi
Shahmaghsoudi

 M.T.O. Shahmaghsoudi® Publications

M.T.O. Shahmaghsoudi®Publications

Sufism and Faith

Nader Angha

Pir, Oveyssi

Library of Congress Control Number: 2003109801

ISBN: 0-910735-75-1

For information regarding our publications please contact:

M.T.O. Publications
6680 Alhambra Ave., PMB 110
Martinez, CA 94553
U.S.A.
E-mail: Publications.us@mto.org
Tel: 1-877-MTO-4YOU (1-877-686-4968)
Tel/Fax: 925-933-2262

Printed by:

M.T.O. Shahmaghsoudi® Printing Center
10590 Magnolia Ave., Suite G
Riverside, CA 92505
U.S.A.
E-mail: Anghars@pacbell.net
Tel: 1-800-830-0320

Printed in China
First Printing
September 30, 2003

Contents

*When the masculine gender is used,
it is for the purpose of linguistic convenience.
Sufism addresses the soul, the spirit, and
the reality of religion. These are beyond gender.*

Preface

To escape the confines and constraints of one's own physical, cultural, and ethnic background is exceedingly rare. However, Salaheddin Ali Nader Angha, Pir Oveyssi Shahmaghsoudi, has succeeded in moving beyond these boundaries into the vastness of the soul and spirit. Both this and his other works express his all-encompassing, clear view, nourished by both the East into which he was born, the West in which he received his formal higher education, specializing in mathematics and physics, and the expanse of the spiritual realm to which he has ascended.

Gently, quietly, with infinite patience and love, Hazrat Pir teaches others how to also recognize and move beyond their own personal boundaries toward knowledge of their genuine, true self hidden beneath the veils of habit and thought. Discovery of this true self, of the essence of our being, of the "I" that is our center is the goal of Sufism. As the Prophet Mohammad *(peace be upon him)* stated: "Whoever knows the true self, knows the Creator." Also in the seventh century, Amir-al-Moeminin Ali *(peace be upon him)* stated: "Whoever sets right his inward self, God sets right his outward self[1] ."

Hazrat Pir provides the guidance of one who has been there and knows the way to attaining the highest wisdom, for he has lived the experience. For 1400 years, an unbroken succession of spiritual masters have transmitted the tradition from heart to heart, leading seekers through the perils and pitfalls of the spiritual journey. This knowledge has been passed directly from Master to Master over the centuries, so that those women and men who seek to attain the divine state will be guided toward such a goal.

A well-known historical example of the relationship between master and student is Rumi, the 13th century Sufi who is now the best-selling poet in the United States. People, yearning for love, constantly read Rumi's poetry, as if reciting it would provide them his spiritual status. They forget that all Rumi is and all the love poetry he wrote is the result of his loving submission to his teacher, Shams. Before Shams came, Rumi was a run of the mill academic. After Shams arrived, Rumi was enraptured with love. He begged: "When will my heart be enlightened by your light, like the moon shines because of the sun[2] ?" Finally annihilated in his master, he consequently became the ecstatic mystic who could write the love poetry that still fascinates people 700 years later, saying "My heart is like snow, melting every moment." Rumi taught the principle of his own experience, warning us very clearly: "Whoever travels without a guide needs two hundred years for a two days' journey[3] ."

The presence of the Pir differentiates and characterizes Sufism, for the Pir personifies what the seeker wishes to attain. The Pir has always submitted totally to his master, in order to reach a state of purity through which he has attained a direct relationship with God, is united with God, is annihilated in God, so that no other but God is in his heart. His personal ego is demolished, and he is one with the Divine Beloved, God. Having such a wise and knowledgeable guide is of great benefit to the seeker, for the guide always knows the quickest and safest route to the spiritual summit.

Observers of human behavior cannot help but look at outcomes, noting the psychological consequences of the guidance of the Pir. The sincere students of Hazrat Pir escape Thoreau's "lives of quiet desperation", instead leading lives of loving, joyful, creative development. Latent abilities and capabilities, dwelling hidden within each person, emerge and are expressed. It is as if the wellspring of life is tapped, and the positive attributes, the love, hope, goodness, vision, generosity, serenity, intelligence, humor, patience, contentment, kindness, talent,...etc. hidden within every human are finally able to flow freely forth. The new inner awareness is reflected in visible outer calmness, and seekers lead lives of harmony, unity and peace.

The inspired tutelage of Hazrat Pir follows in the footsteps of his father, the world-renowned Master Molana-al-Moazam Hazrat Shah Maghsoud Sadegh Angha. Called Professor Angha by his students, he opened the doors of Sufism, previously offered only to a small number of carefully selected students, to all sincere seekers. Hazrat Pir also continues in the path of his grandfather, Molana Mir Ghotbeddin Mohammad Angha, and his great-grandfather, Molana Jalaleddin Ali Mir Abolfazl Angha in translating traditional Sufi concepts into the language of science. The result has been a dramatic expansion of the School of Islamic Sufism. The Khaneghahs (Centers) of

M.T.O. Shahmaghsoudi now encompass the globe, providing the opportunity for learning to all who seek to discover the Truth.

Numerous seekers longingly echo the words of Hazrat Pir:

Unfold my wings, set me to fly,

From the fortress of these dungeon walls,

My liberation grant [4]

The Editor

Editor's Note: The foundation for this work (Sufism & Faith) was a lecture given at Georgia State University, by Nader Angha in Atlanta, on February 18, 1999.

****

In the name of God
Most Gracious, Most Compassionate

Glory to thy Lord,
The Lord of Honor and Power,
(He is free) From what they ascribe (to Him),
And Peace on the Messengers,
And praise to Allah,
The Lord and Cherisher,
Of The Worlds.

(Holy Qur'an 37:180-182)

"Self image is the veil that covers the soul."

Nader Angha

Laws

Do not attach yourself to any particular creed exclusively so that you may disbelieve in all the rest, otherwise you will lose much; God. Nay, you will fail to recognize the real truth of the matter. God, the Omnipotent is not limited to any one creed, for he says:

Wherever you turn, there is the face of God.

(Holy Qur'an, 2:115)

Throughout the years I have given numerous lectures on physical, mental and spiritual aspects of human behavior which all flourish from the depths of Islamic Sufism. In these lectures I have observed that the audience mainly base their questions and reactions on prefabricated theories, and the influences of their social, cultural and ideological background.

This reaction may be satisfactory on the surface but can not enable the mind to reflect deeper into the subject matter. If we are to gain a better understanding of any topic, we have to look at that topic with an open mind and seek to gain a broader outlook on it rather than follow certain patterns, laws or rules or worry about what others may think or say.

People usually think in terms of two kinds of laws. People often call the laws governing the behavior of non-living physical objects Laws of Nature. Classes in physics describe many of these laws, which include the laws of gravity, motion, energy, etc. It is a law of nature that the sun will rise every morning and set every evening. The motion of the tides is a law of nature, as are the orbits of the shining stars we see at night. These laws are not man-made. Yet if there is a law, there must be a Lawmaker. These natural laws or laws of nature must have a grander Lawmaker than do our man-made laws.

We think these physical events will continue forever, but change is ever present. The universe is slowly expanding; stars are formed and fade away, their lives defined by a time scale far beyond our puny experience. We usually are unaware of living by these laws, but if they did not exist, neither would we. For example, the energy of the sun sustains our planet and everything upon it. Without the sun, we would perish.

In everyday life, if someone says "laws", we usually think of lawyers and of lawmakers, of the rulers or legislators who make the laws. But the laws or rules by which humans live are the object of study by many fields in addition to the legal profession. Innumerable man-made laws govern our lives, and we are often not even aware they exist. "Laws" do not have to be written into a formal document to be very powerful and very well enforced.

In every arena of life, there are laws, from the family to all the social institutions. Every occupation has its own rules about how one must behave in that field of work. Most of the laws are informal, but in certain professions formal codes of ethics govern behavior. I would like to take a few minutes to explore the different laws that govern our lives, starting with laws in families.

Family Laws

Every family develops its own sets of laws, or rules, about how one behaves both within the family and toward those outside the family. Often these rules are based on, or at least influenced by, the rules of the larger society. For example, in some families, little emotionality is displayed. In other families, emotions are frequently and perhaps dramatically expressed. Whatever the family rules are, they are passed on from one generation to the next. A common rule is that whatever occurs within the family, particularly if it is undesirable, is to be kept within the family. No one in the world outside must know. In many families, some individuals feel that they are always right in what they say or do; they therefore disregard any opinions that contradict their own.

Family rules about interactions within the family may be very simple, determining with whom one must spend holidays, or become very complex, indicating precisely the various types of communication appropriate for each member. We are often taught from childhood that one must be in control of all interactions, feelings and personal behavior at all times. Usually control is the major defense strategy to avoid feeling shame. Blame is also used to cover shame. Whenever things don't turn out as planned, someone must be blamed. If it is someone else's fault, then one does not have to feel ashamed or take responsibility for any contribution to the situation.

Family laws may be supportive of individual family members, or have a detrimental effect on the individual members, discouraging development of unique personal talents and capacities. Family laws can encourage individual development or discourage deviation from the family norms. Family laws, colored by societal values, often determine the level of education and what types of education and occupations are appropriate for family members. A professional career or a family business or trade may be the only acceptable option to a family.

These rules are not difficult to maintain, because as children are born into the family, they take both the words and the behavior of their parents to be the truth about reality. Infants and young children naturally imitate the behavior of others. To a child, the parents are their primary models and also their idols, all knowing, and they trust whatever the parents tell or teach them. The result is that most people end up later experiencing disillusionment when in their real life experiences they first discover something their parents have told or taught them is not true or is not the most appropriate approach. When this happens, often there is a feeling of doubt, insecurity and fear that perhaps much of what they have learned may be incorrect or not as they had imagined. Other family members, such as grandparents, aunts, or uncles, may also play an important role in teaching and reinforcing the habitual behavior patterns in the family.

Social Laws

Social laws also play an active role in our lives. Sociologists attempt to study and describe the laws governing the relationships and social organization of all societies. There are different levels and types of laws.

Most, but not all, societies have sets of formal, written laws. These are the "law of the land", and breaking these laws may, and often does, result in formal punishment. For example, you can go to jail. Within larger societies, sub-groups may have Codes of Ethics or Rules of Conduct to which all belonging to the particular group are expected to adhere. For example, physicians, attorneys and psychologists have formal Codes of Ethics.

All societies, without exception, have informal laws. The "punishment" for breaking these social laws is less stringent and more personalized than the punishment for breaking formal laws. For example, most societies have informal laws about differential treatment of varied ethnic groups within the larger society. The leaders in such societies teach that such behavior and the accompanying rules and laws are both appropriate and "right", often mis-using the sacred texts of the society to uphold their beliefs. When formal laws change, the obvious forms of differential treatment disappear, but more subtle, informal forms may still permeate the society[5] .

The informal laws are learned gradually, and govern many aspects of our lives without our even being consciously aware they exist. These laws tell us how it is appropriate to behave with many different people in many different situations. Often people come to recognize their existence for the first time when they visit other countries and observe the differences in the informal laws.

Social laws tell us what is valued by the society, and from these we learn what we should value. For example, the U.S. is famed for its materialistic values, for its emphasis on conspicuous consumption, on accumulating wealth to buy more and more, bigger and bigger, newer and newer, more valuable possessions. These acquisitions are obviously not based on need.

Most people consider themselves exceptions, somehow exempt from the informal laws of their society. They do not like to admit that their society has any personal control over them, preferring to believe that they are personally in control. However, a standard assignment in many Introductory Sociology classes is for students to go out into the community and deliberately break a minor social "law" in an innocuous way where others can observe them doing so. An example would be entering a crowded elevator in a tall building and standing at the front with your back toward the door, facing everyone else and smiling. People quickly become aware of the level of discomfort, even fear, that they experience at simply thinking about breaking a social rule, and the anxiety tends to increase with the actual act.

Nikolai Berdyaev stated: "Of all the forms of slavery to which man is liable, the greatest importance attaches to the slavery of man to society[6]."

Cultural Laws

It is not easy to differentiate between what should best be deemed social and what should be deemed cultural laws. Anthropologists attempt to study the cultural laws of societies, often emphasizing the differences between various cultural groups. Characteristically, members of the "more developed" and hence a group that considers itself more "civilized" are quite condescending, and consider their cultural rules to be far superior, and the rules of more primitive cultures to be quite amusing. However, it is a matter of perspective.

The forms of entertainment and activities are dictated by the culture —— these include the types of athletic events, theater, dance forms, art forms, and particularly the various types of music and musical instruments. Growing up in any particular culture, one "naturally" accepts, receives both informal and formal education regarding, and learns how to appreciate and respond to the forms presented.

How much we touch other people and how close or far apart people stand when communicating are usually cultural dictates which people tend to think of as "natural". Cultural laws determine whether we tend to work collaboratively and co-operatively or competitively. Cultural laws determine the characteristics necessary for those in powerful positions, and the characteristics deemed important vary, sometimes enormously, from culture to culture.

Laws about clothing and make-up styles vary enormously from culture to culture. They also vary depending on the particular social situations and times. We have all seen pictures or examples of clothing from other places and other eras. Yet the personal experience is of the necessity of following the current laws and dressing as is appropriate for the time, place, and cultural group. We follow whatever is the current law for our culture. Those who do not are often mocked by others and may pay a penalty.

Laws about gender roles also vary from culture to culture and time to time. However, every culture assigns specific roles to males and specific roles to females in addition to those behaviors that are dependent upon physiological differences between the sexes, such as nursing children. And in all cultures, whatever roles are assigned to the males are reinforced more strongly, considered more important, and are more valued by the culture.

There are laws governing our personal affairs and behavior as well.

Personal Laws

Psychologists attempt to study the laws governing individual human behavior. Psychologists describe human development as if the physical body is all we are, and describe what happens to us physically from conception to the grave. Obviously, great physical changes do occur. The laws of psychology are based solely on the physical, material aspects of the human, including their relationships with other individuals and the society as a whole. The focus, depending on the theoretical orientation, usually tends to be external, based on overt behaviors and their consequences. Researchers examine concrete behaviors, which are easy to measure, although what matters most may not be so easy to measure.

Personal laws, that is, the habitual behaviors that all of us possess, the rules of behavior we follow from day to day, are the result of the interaction between our genetic inheritance and the reaction of our physical senses to the unique personal environment in which we have been immersed. Personal laws include our particular individual "addictions", whether they be to soda, soccer, sex, alcohol, caffeine, chocolate, cars or shopping.

The most powerful personal laws are the patterns of thinking we use on a daily basis. These thought patterns are like software installed in the biochemical computer of our brain, and all are learned. A child who is constantly criticized will learn how to constantly criticize him or herself. A child who is constantly told how good, wonderful and how beautiful or handsome he or she is will learn how to inflate their own ego with their thought process. How we think determines our emotional response, for our brain is a mediator, interpreting the meaning of any event in our lives and triggering the consequent emotional reaction. What to fear, what to be afraid of, is often a key element in this process.

Most importantly, what we think about is what we actually worship, no matter how different our thoughts are from what we would like to think we believe. Whatever our brain is constantly preoccupied with, whether it be success, possessions, children, obtaining love, or wealth, is our idol. For those few who choose to be preoccupied with the spiritual realm, and work on nourishing and developing their innermost being, the standards of behavior change in a positive direction, for they develop their inner capacities.

Psychology itself ignores the soul or spirit, since it is not quantifiable. As a result, psychology does not know how to enable people to discover and develop their own innate abilities and capacities, and neither does psychotherapy. Some psychologists, such as Abraham Maslow, have recognized that personal development is important, but they have only been able to describe people whom they considered to be highly developed. They do not know how to enable people to attain maximal development.

Psychotherapists try to help people who are suffering mentally or emotionally, who may be disturbed, sad, anxious, fearful, discontented, or unhappy. The laws of psychotherapy and the methods taught by therapists, also deal with the physical, behavioral level. These techniques can be helpful in everyday life, particularly in enabling individuals to change their thinking patterns in a more positive direction. Their primary focus is usually on enabling the individual to be able to function within the society. A notable exception is the work of Jung[7] and a few others, who recognized the importance of the spiritual realm.

Educational Laws

The laws about knowledge are presented through the educational system. An often-accepted definition of the purpose of education is to pass on the accumulated knowledge of the human race. However, only certain kinds of information are presented. Educational systems systematically teach cultural belief systems and emphasize what the particular culture considers important. We teach our children to accept unquestioningly what is taught as truth, yet education consists of learning the ideas of others. Sociologists are quite clear that a major function of schools is to inculcate societal values, beliefs, attitudes and behavioral patterns. They help to maintain social control and ensure the proper occupational roles will be filled[8].

The best educators are keenly aware of the personal consequences of educational systems and criticize them sharply. Anthropologist Jules[9] Henry states:

> The function of education has never been to free the mind and spirit of man, but to bind them; and to the end that the mind and spirit of his children should never escape, Homo sapiens has employed praise, ridicule, admonition, accusation, mutilation and even torture to chain them to the culture pattern. Throughout most of his historic course Homo sapiens has wanted from his children acquiescence, not originality.

Teacher John Holt[10] , the author of the best-selling books, *How Children Learn and How Children Fail,* now advocates home schooling for parents who wish to avoid the robotization of their children.

Paolo Freire[11] , exiled for his success in teaching illiterate peasants, states the case even more strongly:

> ...what happens to a greater or lesser degree in the various "worlds" (cultures) into which the world is divided is that the ordinary person is crushed, diminished, converted into a spectator, maneuvered by myths which powerful social forces have created. These myths turn against him; then destroy and annihilate him.

The public educational system is the primary force in this destruction.

A college education today is essentially the study of the prethought thoughts, the man-made laws governing various fields. Whether one studies physics, music, chemistry, mathematics or art, the laws of that particular field, based on the ideas of previous people in that field, are taught. Many college majors deal with the laws of specific aspects of human behavior. Psychologists study the laws of both individual behavior and family behavior. Sociologists study the laws of various levels of social groups and their relationships toward each other. Anthropologists study the laws characterizing various cultures. Political scientists study the laws of political systems. Huge schools of business teach the rules by which businesses and corporations are run within this particular society. Ethnic studies and women's studies courses teach the rules that are followed in relation to these particular sub-groups. They all describe what is observed, they all teach prethought thoughts.

Focus in the Western educational system is on job preparation, providing students whatever laws are needed to enter their chosen occupation. Students are forced to specialize at earlier and earlier ages, then spend additional years beyond college in ever-increasing narrowness of focus. People are educated to follow the man-made laws, to consider knowing the thoughts of others to be the epitome of knowledge.

Conformity

The areas previously listed are only a brief overview of the different laws that govern our daily lives. People live enmeshed in these man-made informal laws which constrain, limit, and bound us. The laws of our family, culture, and society tell us what to do and how to do it at every moment, from what to eat and what to think, to how to move. Very few ever recognize that they are imprisoned by these laws, although the language is peppered with trite sayings describing conformity. People are said to: "keep up with the Joneses", "join the parade", "play the game", "follow the beaten path", "follow suit", "run with the pack", or "follow the crowd". Very few ever break free. Very few ever discover their own innate talents and capabilities. Freire states that:

> There is no such thing as a neutral educational
> process. Either education is an instrument to

enforce conformity,...or it becomes the practice of freedom, the means by which men and women deal critically and creatively with reality and discover how to participate in the transformation of their world[12] .

Fear is commonly used as a tool to ensure conformity to these laws. We teach fear to our kids from the day they are born: "Don't do that because it will hurt you," and so on, so they grow up with the sense of fear and anxiety and fear gradually comes to permeate their existence. In their adulthood, in respect to any decisionmaking, they attempt it with fear, and not with the proper way of thinking or knowledge. They fear change, censure, controversy, loss. Most of all, they fear death as children fear the dark. "Death in itself is nothing; but we fear to be we know not what, we know not where."[13] This fear is one rule among others they carry throughout their lives. Yet Bacon told us that nothing is terrible except fear itself, and Thoreau echoed this sentiment, stating, "Nothing is so much to be feared as fear."[14]

The result is that many individuals are lost, confused or lack stability in this life. Often these individuals have no sense of direction and no sense of purpose. Although they may think they are successful in their careers and lives, their happiness is often limited to momentary phases gained from obtaining physical or material things. They develop a want and satisfy it, then develop another want in an endless succession of desires whose satisfaction never brings more than momentary pleasure. Success in material objects does not provide them with true happiness, so they often feel that there is something missing in their life. Having achieved the goals society has taught them they should pursue, they ask: "Is this all there is?" They feel empty and at times in despair when faced with hardship in everyday life. Often they may view life as unfair, filled with pain and suffering. They look around them and view the world as one filled with disease, poverty, pain, suffering, greed, violence and death. Life in the universe may come to be viewed as sad and painful.

Knowledge

I ask you, if the universe is so bad, how did human beings ever come to attribute it to the work of an All-Wise, All-Merciful and Benevolent Creator? Indeed, how easy and simple it is for man to say these few words: "The cruel and unjust universe!" Being a mathematician I often compare this to simple concepts in mathematics that require so much proof and facts. A man does not call a line crooked unless he has some definition or knowledge of a straight line. What was he comparing this universe with when he called it unjust?

The spectacle of the universe, as revealed by physical experience, could never have been the ground for true spirituality and religion. The foundation must have been something existing in spite of religious institutions, acquired from a different source, not the input from our physical senses or man-made laws.

Despite all the rules which society imposes upon us, the urge to know is inherent in each human being. It is very obvious in young children, and continues through our life span. The quest for the meaning of life, for self-knowledge, for eternity, is timeless. It is not unique to any particular race, creed or culture, nor bound to any particular place.

The Prophets and great Teachers through human history have taught: Know yourself. As I stated in another book:

> Know the "being" who is everlasting and not restricted to the body, to desires, and all the action and reaction that takes place continuously. Know the "being" who is your true identity, the source of your becoming, the source of knowledge, so you may live in peace and balance, so you may know your eternity[15].

Knowing yourself is necessary in order to find truth. The discovery of truth is not the task for the immature mind, nor does it consist of the common comparisons and inputs of the senses to the brain. However, cognition of truth is possible by the light of faith and heart discovery. "It has been said: 'God opens the hearts of the pure and reveals to His believers the true light of faith.[16]'" The light of faith illumines the truth.

When one comes across any topic through one or more of the senses, the immediate response would be to refer them to the information which has been gathered in the mind up to that moment. The memory bank is consulted. The more information, knowledge and experience one has, the more one would have understanding and awareness of the actuality of the subject. Findings based upon knowledge and experience are reliable and trustworthy. But if one depended on the theoretical aspects alone (what he has only heard or read) and has no personal knowledge of the subject, one's finding and comments would be untrustworthy. Ansari prayed: "O God, teach us to recognize knowledge: Light a lamp lest we remain in darkness."[17]

The journey to one's inner realm and the state of one's spirit and soul is not possible by following or studying the thoughts of materialists, who focus only on physical aspects. Nor is it possible through research in the fields of science, which focus on that which is measurable with the physical senses or some extension of their capacities, because they do not provide practical and positive solutions to the needs of contemporary man. The human is so much more than just a biological phenomenon. Partial and limited knowledge of the individual does not contain the hidden references and symbolism of the enlightened, because the limited brain is dependent on the senses in order to understand the outer manifestations of events, to form and understand concepts. It is incapable of differentiating between good and evil, truth and falsehood, because its sole source of knowledge is the input it receives from the physical comparisons, effects and qualities of nature through nature.

"Knowledge is not acquired through study, but is a light that God shines in the heart of he whom He wills."[18] Knowledge manifest in the universe results in stability and peace. If you do not have knowledge of something, repetition will be of no value. Repetition of any word creates images in the mind, which are linked to cultural, social, environmental, political, economical factors. People often repeat the words the Prophets have spoken, thinking that somehow they too have the same knowledge because they repeat the words. But singing his Psalms does not give one the spiritual ascendancy of David. "I may know God, and I may tell you that God is real, and that you can see God, and that you can be in communication with God, but that is my experience."[19] You can repeat what I say a million times, but the experience is still mine, and is not yours. Repeating the word "knowledge" will not give you the vast experience contained in the word. Repeating the word "faith" will not have any reality for you, if you have not gone through the experience.

Sufism

Since the 1990's there has been a fresh interest in mysticism. Sufism is generally considered the mystical dimension of Islam. The word mysticism is often used as a term of mere reproach, to throw at any opinion which we regard as vague, vast and sentimental without any basis in either fact or logic. I would like to present Sufism to you the way I have experienced it.

For thousands of years Sufism has offered a path in which one can progress towards the "great end" of self-realization, or the cognition of God. Sufism is the way of love, a way of devotion and a way of knowledge. It is also called The Way of the Prophets, for it recognizes and respects all the prophets, including Moses, Buddha, Jesus and Mohammad. The universal message of Sufism is that not only love but also self-knowledge leads to knowledge of God. My father, the great Sufi Master of our time, has said:

Real self-knowledge consists in knowing the following:

- **What are you in yourself, and where did you come from?**

- **Where are you going, and for what purpose are you here?**

According to the tradition of Sufism, the reality of humanity and the answers to the above cannot be revealed nor transferred through words or found in books.

Sufis find God by knowing Him, but their mode of knowing is intuitive rather then informational. Sufism represents cognition and awareness. Cognition and awareness in this sense means discovering God through heart discovery and inner vision, rather than through reasoning and deduction. To the Sufis this discovery is not vague or imaginative, but rather it is a personal religious experience that has its roots and center in states of consciousness.

Sufism is the body, soul and spirit of Islam. Sufism is, as I have said for the first time, the "reality of religion". By this I mean experiencing God in one's inner self, submitting to Him and loving Him with one's mind, heart and soul. Sufism, as I know it, is the reality of religion.

Symbolically, the goal of Sufism is union with God. Sufi Masters have often described this union as like a drop of water becoming one with the ocean. When the drop of water loses its boundaries in the ocean's depths, the drop is no longer a separate drop of water, but it is one with the ocean. Like the drop, the lover of God is annihilated in union with the Beloved. Union provides Enlightenment.

To know what a Sufi speaks about, one must experience the same. The truth of the personal experience exists for the individual self who has completed the journey, but for no one else. Sufis have often described this feeling as confined to no terms, no means, no comparison, and no words. They receive the knowledge of God clothed in none of the kinds of images, in none of the sensible representations which our mind makes use of in other circumstances. Accordingly, in this knowledge, since the senses are not employed, they receive neither form nor impression, nor are they able to give an account or furnish any likeness, although the wisdom of the experience is felt so clearly in their innermost soul.

Sufism teaches seekers that true communication about any experience, mystical or otherwise, must be based on shared inner experiences that are grounded in accurate cognition of our situation. Sufism instructs humanity that "things are not as they seem" because we pay attention only to the surface of things with our senses and scattered energy. "Words do not convey the meaning."[31] For example, if you are lost in the burning desert, dying of thirst, with a parched throat, dry mouth, and cracked lips, will receiving the word "water" printed on a piece of paper satisfy your thirst? Of course not. You need the real thing, the reality of water, and only when you receive it will your thirst be satisfied.

Faith

People are good learners, and learn well the various types of informal, unwritten laws previously discussed. People learn from families, their education, their culture, and their society, and from these develop personal laws of habit and thought. The underlying belief is that if one conforms to these laws, then all will be well in life. People believe in the laws that were learned, and conform to them. To do so is to place one's faith in the beliefs and behavior of others. This is the basic belief of humanism, that the answers to the perplexing questions of life are to be found in other people. However, believing the words and behavior of other people, conforming to the informal laws, does not provide harmony, unity, contentment, joy and inner peace.

In sufism, there is one law that is essential, and that is the Law of God, the Lawmaker. The Law of God cannot be learned through the words or dictates of others, nor through the thought processes in the human brain. As Rumi Stated, "The sea will be the sea, whatever the drop's philosophy." The Law of God can only be learned through individual experience of the Divine Beloved. When one has experience, one knows, and consequently has true Faith.

The way of Sufism is The way of the Prophets, and the Prophets, in both Holy books, The Qur'an and The Bible are quite clear and specific in stating the necessity of letting go of all the familial, cultural and social laws and attachments.

The Holy Qur'an, in sura 9:24, states:

Say: if it be that your fathers, your sons, your brothers, your mates, or your kindred; the wealth that you have gained; the commerce in which ye fear a decline; or the dwellings in which ye delight — are dearer to you than God, or His Apostle, or the striving in His cause — then wait until God brings about His decision: And God guides not the rebellious.

A story by Rumi is illustrative. In the story, a salik (truth-seeker) is told by his Sufi Master to bring him a bottle of wine. The salik says he is afraid that the townspeople will attack him when they see him, a supposedly devout Muslim, coming through town with a bottle of wine, which Muslims are forbidden to drink. The Master tells him to bring the wine, nevertheless. The fearful salik buys the wine, and sure enough, the townspeople attack him, at first verbally, then physically. At that point, the bottle is broken, and found to contain vinegar, not wine, and the salik is "saved" from the townspeople, but is ashamed before his Master because he did not complete his task (Rumi, 1926).

The seeker was governed by social laws, by fear of what other people would think, and lacked faith in his spiritual teacher. To fully understand the story, one needs to know that in Sufism, wine is often used as a symbolic reference to the living Presence of the Divine. *In Al Rasa'el,* Professor Angha, in describing the journey toward the States of Enlightenment, states:

> At this time, for the esteemed and the chosen, the
> soul's cup is filled solely with the clearest, purifying,
> divine wine, the eternal wine of His glorious
> presence, blessed by the touch of His Magnificent
> Countenance, the ever eternal wine of blissful Light
> for the circle of those yearning for the Face and
> Eyes of the Bearer of Wine.

And so the seeker, who was sent for the blessed divine wine, instead received the vinegar resulting from social relationships. Each of us has to make the choice between socio/cultural laws and the Law of God, and we make choices on a daily basis, from moment to moment. The choice is between wine and vinegar. One chooses to have faith in social and personal constructs or to have faith in God. If one chooses faith in God, the question then remains as to how true faith can be attained.

Faith and religion are two terms that often get confused and exchanged for one another. People may say, "I am of the Baptist faith.", or "My faith is Buddhism." The standard dictionary definition typically mirrors this confusion. It states faith is derived from the Latin word for trust. It then describes faith both as trust in something, and as religion, in addition to other meanings[20]. A typical thesaurus divides the synonyms for faith into two categories, one of complete trust and the other of a formal system of beliefs.[21] Internet websites and titles of books in print repeat this pattern. Although the terms faith and religion are interdependent, they are not synonymous. Faith is the belief and trust in something such as God. Al-Hujwiri writes that real faith is trust in God.[22]

Religion is an expression of Faith, with religious institutions usually including a creed, code and cult. Jews, Christians and Muslims all believe in One God and in the prophets, but each group has a different creed, code and cult. Religious traditions need Faith or they become empty, a meaningless repetition of ritual. Faith needs religious avenues in order to express itself. Today it seems as though religious institutions influence faith as much as faith influences religious institutions. Both influence how we view the world and the meaning we give to life.

However, faith among people is generally based on

acceptance of the edicts of religious institutions, without question. In this regard, God is worshiped because of our endless needs, our fear of punishment and hell or the desire for Paradise. This is blind faith, and not faith based on cognition. However, the faith that the prophets experienced and have spoken of is quite different. It is based on cognition and certain knowledge. Then one becomes,"One in whom persuasion and belief has ripened into faith, and faith become a passionate intuition."[23]

Knowledge and faith differ in meaning and experience for different people. Knowledge and faith are thought to be adjacent, one involving the seen, the other the unseen. Khafif says:

> "Faith is the belief of the heart in that knowledge which comes from the Unseen," because faith is in that which is hidden, and it can be attained only through Divine strengthening of one's certainty, which is the result of knowledge bestowed by God.[24]

However, if one considers the experiential aspects of the teachings of the prophets, it becomes quite evident that true faith is grounded in knowledge. The prophets have spoken of God in a highly personal and intimate manner. They have spoken of God as the Father, the Beloved, the Omnipotent, the Eternal,...etc., which means that they could hear God, they could see God, and they had experienced God. One could take the position that it was the power of their faith that propelled them to speak so strongly and not the actual seeing and hearing that took place. But one should ask: What was the foundation of their faith? In other words, one can worship God as if one saw God, which is the common way of worship. Or one can see God, experience God, and then worship God, which is the way of the prophets, the saints and the Sufis.

True faith is an inner summons. True faith is a process whereby a seal from one's heart is lifted and one is able to witness the "Unseen". It is in the witnessing of the "Unseen" that one's faith becomes firmly rooted in knowledge. In other words, true faith is a process whereby the hidden mysteries of existence are revealed to the seeker. When faith is established, the seeker submits to the will of God and begins the journey on the path of self-knowledge. This is the goal of, and the essence of Sufism.

If there were no light in the universe, we would never know it was dark. Dark would be a word without meaning. But there is light.

God is the light of the heavens and of the earth;

The parable of His Light is as if there were a Niche,

And within it a Lamp;

The Lamp enclosed in Glass;

The Glass as it were a brilliant Star;

lit from a blessed Tree,

An Olive, neither of the East nor of the West,

Whose Oil is well-nigh luminous,

Though the fire scarce touched it,

Light upon Light!

God doth guide whom He will to His Light,

God doth set forth parables for men;

and God doth know all things.

(Holy Qur'an 24:35)

God is the protector of those who have faith;

from the depths of darkness He leads them forth into light.

(Holy Qur'an 2:257)

Faith could be described as strong belief in something, sometimes even without proof. Everyone has faith in something or someone. For example one might have absolute faith that the sun will rise tomorrow. Sir William Osler stated: "Nothing in life is more wonderful than faith—the one great moving force which we can neither weigh in the balance nor test in the crucible."[25] the complete trust certainly and conviction of faith can produce profound results. Faith has healing power, described in diverse sources, including modern medical research on the placebo effect. If we recognize the value and strength of faith within us, we will experience a feeling of relief and gradually everything that we come across in our daily life will become easier. We become content in life and experience inner happiness. "It is He who sent down tranquility into the hearts of the believers that they may add faith to their faith. For to God belong the forces of the heavens and earth, and God is the source of knowledge and wisdom (Holy Qur'an, 48:4)."

Have faith in your ability and your potential as you would in God. Waitley called such faith a seed of greatness. The power of the ability and potential in man does not become less or less valuable in any case of distraction or disaster. The essence of your life is an ocean with no ending.

Let your spirit in His solitude travel to the jewel of knowledge, which is within you, and excavate the vastness of that knowledge. To make sure that indecisiveness and doubt do not interfere, learn to gain control of your mind. Peace is one of the fruits of being decisive and is based on complete faith and understanding of experience. When we have inner peace we can generally experience freedom and be in control of our mind. Then we are "on top of the world". When we recognize the sources of power within ourselves then we will reach the central source of our life. The Holy Qur'an states: "It is those who believe and confuse not their beliefs with wrong   that are in security, for they are on guidance (6:82)."

The Lord of the believers, Ali *(peace be upon him)* has said: "Faith is manifested in the heart as a ray of light, and as faith increases, the light spreads."[27] This ray of light is the source of life in the heart; it is human reality and the fountain of eternal knowledge. And he has also said: "The heart is an open book."[28] Faith is belief of the heart in whatever knowledge is revealed and taught to it from the unseen world, and the beholding of the glory and presence of God.

> ...Believers are those who, when God is mentioned, feel a tremor in their hearts, and when they hear His revelations rehearsed, find their faith strengthened, and put their trust in their Lord.
>
> *(Holy Qur'an, 8:2)*

> "...God has endeared the faith to you, and has made it beautiful in your hearts...."
>
> *(Holy Qur'an, 49:7)*

Faith is the fruit of certainty. Certainty is trust in the unseen for elimination of doubt. If certainty is achieved through reasoning, it is called *elm-al-yaghin* (definite knowledge), if seen by the eye through the conscious innate wisdom common to all life, it is *ayn-al-yaghin* (experimental knowledge), and if it is set first in the realm of the manifestation of the attributes and secondly in the light of the manifestation of reality, it is *hagh-al-yaghin* (true knowledge).

Faith and devotion are qualities that gain control over the heart, disposing it to comply with the commands to which it is required to submit. The Holy Prophet has said: "Faith is not achieved for the asking, but settles in the heart and is confirmed by action." Faith comes from purity of heart and annihilation of the self in the Exalted Lord and is obtained through cognition; is obtained in witnessing the Lord through the heart, because the pure heart is the place for God's presence and His blessings.

The soul of the Sufi is not concerned with reward, but rather attunement to the will of God. When your motive is to serve God alone and when you allow the Divine Will to flow through your consciousness, great joy results. We are here to learn and grow. "For the purpose of this way there is no comrade more faithful than works. If they be good they will be your friends forever, and if they be evil they will be as a snake in thy tomb," said the Prophet Mohammad *(peace be upon him)*. Furthermore, He said: "Whoever has no livelihood does not have eternity." **We must also act.**

Einstein stated: "Whatever there is of God and goodness in the universe, it must work itself out and express itself through us. We cannot stand aside and let God do it."[29]

Rumi, in *Masnavi* [30] , has said:

Act and word are witnesses to the hidden mind;

From these twain infer the inward state.

The word-witness is rejected if it speaks falsely,

And the act-witness is rejected if it does not run straight.

Thou must have words and acts that are not

self-contradictory,

In order that thou may meet with immediate acceptance.

Conclusion

In conclusion, Sufism is the reality of religion. It is based on the reality of your "being", the stable and constant element of your existence. It is not imaginary, it cannot be inherited, and it cannot be forced nor enforced. In essence, it is a method, a way, a discipline that teaches each person the science of exploring one's own being, unearthing one's hidden talent and potentials, and discovering the reality of being in this unbounded and infinite tapestry called existence. If we look closely at the human being, we cannot but be amazed and in awe of this exquisite and unique masterpiece of creation, operated by the will of knowledge, whose silent hand has unwrapped the potential of being into manifestations, so that the pages of existence may be adorned with the beauty of its wisdom.

Hazrat Mir Ghotbeddin Mohammed Angha, Pir, Oveyssi, my grandfather, has said; "If only the alphabet of the one spiritual book were revealed to man, and the secret of the soul discovered, he would need none of the words sealed in silent books, and yet would know the story whole." [32]

Peace and tranquility can never be realized unless each human being is educated to discover the laws governing their being. By education I mean "innate endowed knowledge." Sufism can provide a haven for the positive spiritual development of each individual, which can transform each being and lead their soul to the gates of their true faith. We read in the Holy Qur'an: "It is neither their flesh nor their blood that reaches God: it is your devotion that reaches Him." (22:37)

I would like to conclude with a poem from the famous Sufi poet Rumi:

What is the solution, O Moslem,

For I do not know myself,

Neither Christian, Jew, Zoroastrian nor Moslem am I,

I am not an Easterner or a Westerner or of land or sea,

Not of nature, not of heaven, not of India, or China,

My place is placelessness, my sign is no sign,

I have no body or life, for I am of the life of life,

I have put away duality, I have seen the two worlds as one,

I desire One, I know One, I see One, I call One (God) [33.]

Let us light the candle of understanding in our heart,
Which shall not be put out.

NOTES

[1] Quoted in Wilcox, Lynn (1998). *Sayings of the Sufi Sages.* M.T.O. Publications.

[2] Rumi, Mevlana Celaleddin (1995). *Divan-I Kebir (Vol. 1)* Translated by Nevit Ogus Ergin. Turkish Republic Ministry of Culture and Current.

[3] Rumi, Jalalu'ddin (1930). *The Mathnawi of Jalalu'ddin Rumi* (Book IV). Edited and translated by Reynold A. Nicholson. Gibb Memorial Trust.

[4] Angha, Nader (1989). *The Approaching Promise.* University Press of America, p. 8.

[5] See Sleek, Scott (1999). Three Decades after King, Report Card. *APA Monitor,* 30,(1), 24.

[6] Berdyaev, Nikolai (1944). *Slavery and Freedom.* Charles Scribner's Sons. p. 102.

[7] Jung, Carl Gustav (1933). *Modern Man in Search of a Soul.* Harcourt, Brace & World; (1938). *Psychology and Religion.* Yale University Press. (1971). *The Portable Jung.* Penguin.

[8] Rioedan, Cornelius (1997). *Equality and Achievement*: An Introduction to the Sociology of Education, Addison-Wesley.

[9] Henry, Jules (1969). In Suburban Classrooms. In Gross, Beatrice & Ronald. *Radical School Reform.* Simon & Schuster.

[10] Holt, John (1995). *How Children Learn* (rev. ed.). Perseus Press. (1995). *How Children Fail* (rev. ed.). Perseus Press.

[11] Freire, Paulo (1973). *Education for Critical Consciousness.* Perseus Press.

[12] Freire, Paulo (1995). *Pedagogy of the Oppressed* (20th rev. ed.) Continuum.

[13] Dryden, John (1676). *Aureng-Zebe.* Act. IV, Sc.I.

[14] Bacon, Francis. *DeAugmentis Scientiarium*, Book II and Thoreau, Henry David. *Journal.* Sept. 7, 1851.

[15] Angha, Nader (1995). *Sufism and Knowledge.* Riverside, CA: MTO Publications. p.18.

[16] Angha, Shah Maghsoud Sadegh (1986). *Al-Rasa'el.* University Press of America.

[17] Ansari, Kwaja Abdullah (1978). *Intimate Conversations.* New York: Paulist Press.

[18] *Al-Rasa'el.*

[19] *Sufism and Knowledge.*

[20] *Webster's New Universal Unabridged Dictionary* (1989). New York: Barnes & Noble.

[21] Laird, Chatlton (1985). *Webster's New World Thesaurus.* New York: Simon and Schuster.

[22] Al-Hujwiri, (1911-1999). *Revelation of the Mystery.* Accord, NY: Pir Press.

[23] Wordsworth, William (1814). *The Excursion.* Bk. 1, line 1293

[24] *Revelation of the Mystery*, p. 290.

[25] Quoted in Cushing, Harvey (1925). *The Life of Sir William Osler.* V. 2, p. 30.

[26] Angha, Shah Maghsoud Sadegh. Quoted in Angha, Nader (1996). *The Fragrance of Sufism.* University Press of America, p. xxi.

[27] Ali, Amir al Mu'menin (1980). *Nahj al-Balaghah.* World Organization for Islamic Services.

[28]Ibid.

[29] Einstein, Albert (1940). Conversation recorded by Algernon Black. Einstein Archive 54-834.

[30] Rumi, Jalaluddin (1930). *The Mathnawi of Jalalu'ddin Rumi.* Gibb Memorial Trust. Vol. 6, p. 17.

[31]Angha, Shah Maghsoud Sadegh (1991). *Dawn.* M.T.O. Publications.

[32]Angha, Mir Ghotbeddin Mohammad. (quoted in Angha, Shah Maghsoud Sadegh (1997). *Manifestations of Thought.* M.T.O. Shahmaghsoudi Publications. p. 1.

[33]Rumi, Jalaluddin (1979). E.H. Whinfield (Ed.). *Selections from Divan Shams Tabriz.* Translated by Idries Shah. Octagon Press.

Genealogy of Maktab Tarighat Oveyssi Shahmaghsoudi ®
(School of Islamic Sufism)

Prophet Mohammad
Imam Ali

1. Hazrat Oveys Gharani*
2. Hazrat Salman Farsi
3. Hazrat Habib-ibn Salim Ra'i
4. Hazrat Soltan Ebrahim Adham
5. Hazrat Abu Ali Shaghigh Balkhi
6. Hazrat Sheikh Abu Torab Nakhshabi
7. Hazrat Sheikh Abu Amr Estakhri
8. Hazrat Abu Ja'far Hazza
9. Hazrat Sheikh Kabir Abu Abdollah Mohammad-ibn Khafif Shirazi
10. Hazrat Sheikh Hossein Akkar
11. Hazrat Sheikh Morshed AbuIsshaq Shahriar Kazerouni
12. Hazrat Khatib Abolfath Abdolkarim
13. Hazrat Ali-ibn Hassan Basri
14. Hazrat Serajeddin Abolfath Mahmoud-ibn Mahmoudi Sabouni Beyaavi
15. Hazrat Sheikh Abu Abdollah Rouzbehan Baghli Shirazi
16. Hazrat Sheikh Najmeddin Tamat-al-Kobra Khaivaghi
17. Hazrat Sheikh Ali Lala Ghaznavi
18. Hazrat Sheikh Ahmad Zaker Jowzeghani
19. Hazrat Noureddin Abdolrahman Esfarayeni
20. Hazrat Sheikh Alaoddowleh Semnani
21. Hazrat Mahmoud Mazdaghani
22. Hazrat Amir Seyyed Ali Hamedani
23. Hazrat Sheikh Ahmad Khatlani
24. Hazrat Seyyed Mohammad Abdollah Ghatifi-al-Hasavi Nourbakhsh
25. Hazrat Shah Ghassem Feyzbakhsh

26. Hazrat Hossein Abarghoui Janbakhsh
27. Hazrat Darvish Malek Ali Joveyni
28. Hazrat Darvish Ali Sodeyri
29. Hazrat Darvish Kamaleddin Sodeyri
30. Hazrat Darvish Mohammad Mozahab Karandehi (Pir Palandouz)
31. Hazrat Mir Mohammad Mo'men Sodeyri Sabzevari
32. Hazrat Mir Mohammad Taghi Shahi Mashhadi
33. Hazrat Mir Mozaffar Ali
34. Hazrat Mir Mohammad Ali
35. Hazrat Seyyed Shamseddin Mohammad
36. Hazrat Seyyed Abdolvahab Naini
37. Hazrat Haj Mohammad Hassan Kouzekanani
38. Hazrat Agha Abdolghader Jahromi
39. Hazrat Jalaleddin Ali Mir Abolfazl Angha
40. Hazrat Mir Ghotbeddin Mohammad Angha
41. Hazrat Molana Shah Maghsoud Sadegh Angha
42. Hazrat Salaheddin Ali Nader Angha

*The conventional Arabic Transliteration is Uwais al-Qarani

For information regarding
Maktab Tarighat Oveyssi Shahmaghsoudi® School of
Islamic Sufism,
please contact:

M.T.O.Shamaghsoudi® Headquarters
5101 Wisconsin Avenue. N.W., Suite 230
Washington D.C., 20016 U.S.A
1-800-820-2180

website: www.mtoshahmaghsoudi.org